LATE NIGHT LESSONS FROM THE COVID-19 CRISIS.

HOW BUSINESSES, GOVERNMENTS, AND INDIVIDUALS SURVIVED AND THRIVED THROUGH A GLOBAL PANDEMIC. PART 1: 2020 (2ND EDITION).

JON KEY

KEY AND CO LTD

Copyright © 2021 by Jon Key.

All rights reserved. No part of this book may be reproduced or used in any manner without written permission of the copyright owner except for the use of quotations in a book review. For more information, address: corporate@keyand.co.

SECOND EDITION

www.keyandco.org.

❦ Created with Vellum

To the key workers.

Truth is stranger than fiction, but it is because fiction is obliged to stick to possibilities; truth isn't.

– Mark Twain

CONTENTS

Introduction xi

1. Making trade-offs 1
2. Purpose 6
3. Leadership 10
4. Customer relationships 16
5. Planning 22
6. Innovation 26
7. Human resources 32
8. Motivated teams 36
9. Resilience 42
10. Collaboration 46
11. Well-being 50
12. Coming out of lockdown 56
    Bonus chapter: The final lockdown? 60

Epilogue 67
Acknowledgments 69
About the Author 71
Getting in touch 73

"It is not the strongest of the species that survives, nor the most intelligent. It is the one that is the most adaptable to change."

– Charles Darwin

INTRODUCTION

This book is written for anyone who was affected by the COVID-19 crisis – which is to say, everyone on the planet!

Reflection is important to moving forward, and we all have much to reflect on since the virus first struck. Whether you are leading a business, working as an employee, playing a role on the front line, or are simply an observer of the decisions that businesses, governments, and individuals are making, this book is intended to help you to reflect on the recent past and think ahead to the phase ahead of us.

I have an extensive network of clients and associates that I have worked with over the decades. For my network, 2020 was a year of extraordinary challenges as the entire world determined how they would respond to the pandemic spread of COVID-19. How would they continue to make a living or keep their doors open? What tactics and strategies are available to keep their ships afloat?

Coronaviruses are a group of viruses that can be transmitted between animals and people, causing illnesses that may range from the common cold to more severe respiratory syndromes. COVID-19 is a novel coronavirus that had not previously been identified in humans. The virus is highly transmissible, and thousands of new cases are being reported around the world each day. Coughing and sneezing are believed to be the most common forms of transmission. The first case was detected in the Hubei province of China at the end of December 2019.

In February 2020, the International Committee on Taxonomy of Viruses and the World Health Organization announced official names for both the virus and the disease it causes: SARS-CoV-2 and COVID-19, respectively. The name of the disease is derived from the words *corona*, *virus*, and *disease*, while the number 19 represents the year that it emerged.

Before the pandemic, my network of independent consultants was working with businesses, both small and large, public and private, across numerous industries and around the world. We were often tasked with helping them overcome their most pressing issues while also being "flies on the wall" as we observed how CEOs and leadership teams came to terms with COVID-19. We offered insight as we watched them weigh their options and make the difficult but necessary decisions to navigate the crisis.

As events of the year unfolded, my network – like so many others – hosted frequent video conference calls to share our experiences and the types of things we were observing. In these calls, we discussed everything including: making complex and difficult trade-offs, purpose, effective leadership, customer relationships, planning, innovation, human resources, motivating teams, resilience, collaboration, employee and leadership well-being, and preparing for coming out of lockdown.

The clients in the Key and Co. network included global logistics businesses who supplied the world, technology companies who kept it connected, global commodity busi-

INTRODUCTION

nesses distributing essential resources, banks who provided cash and financial services, national health services who treated the sick, retailers who sold crucial groceries, and utilities who kept the heat and lights on and the water flowing.

Many of these video calls stretched late into the evening. They served as a source of support, inspiration, and innovation for both me and everyone involved. The findings of these discussions and late-night video chats were distilled and published online in a series of posts across various platforms.

This book is a compilation of these posts.

I published this book in a fairly raw form to reflect the tone of the year we endured while also ensuring I was to deliver it to as broad of an audience as quickly as possible. Since the first edition, I have updated the text to include some further reflections and added an extra chapter on the UK lockdown during January 2021. I hope you find it not only interesting and thought-provoking but that you take some useful lessons from it as we all enter the next – hopefully optimistic – phase of this global crisis.

"Every decision brings with it some good, some bad, some lessons, and some luck. The only thing that's for sure is that indecision steals many years from many people who wind up wishing they'd just had the courage to leap."

— Doe Zantamata

MAKING TRADE-OFFS

The COVID-19 crisis has brought the need to make difficult trade-offs. Governments had to balance opening the economy with keeping people safe, and lockdowns with financial support. Businesses had to balance their day-to-day survival with investing in their futures and managing their costs while retaining talent. Individuals and families had to balance staying safe while educating children and putting food onto the table.

Trade-offs were already particularly difficult to make and were even more challenging during a period where there has been such a high degree of uncertainty. Governments, businesses, and individuals have never experienced times like these before. Further, there has been a poor, albeit improving, level of information to make decisions from. Trade-offs during the crisis have, largely, come down to judgement.

Non-financial factors had to be considered. Factors like livelihoods, employee well-being, and the number of lives that could be saved. How do you quantify these factors against financial outcomes? What is the cost of saving human lives? The value of children's educations? Of employee mental well-being? Is it even possible to place a financial value on saving lives?

How do you compare the outcome of saving the lives of one group over those of another?

The stakes have never been higher. The gulf between getting it right and wrong is enormous. Getting it wrong means people die, businesses fail, and individuals suffer. But getting it right saves lives and businesses while maintaining individual well-being and prosperity. The difference between how governments have handled the trade-offs has been stark. Some, such as Taiwan, reduced the death toll while maintaining their economy. According to Worldometer coronavirus data, Taiwan had only 7 deaths throughout the whole of 2020 and its economy grew by 3%. Others have succeeded in achieving one but not the other. Some, such as Brazil, the UK and the US, failed on both counts, with almost a billion deaths across just these three countries by February 2021.

The trade-offs during the crisis were not ones that could be avoided. While decision-making was extremely difficult, tough decisions had to be made. Decisions were time-critical, complex, and needed to be made very quickly.

The basics of making trade-offs have not changed. Despite information being sparse, high levels of uncertainty, and the dire consequences of getting it wrong, it was more important than ever to maintain a rigorous approach to addressing trade-offs that combined data and logic, people, process, and leadership.

Logic, data, and structure helped. Trade-offs were easier when desired outcomes could be agreed upon upfront and framed logically. Comparing the options on the same or a similar basis, in a structured way, helped organizations make the right decisions. This structure was further enhanced when decisions were underpinned with data, allowing for fact-based decisions.

The best examples of trade-offs came when there was a focus on hearts and minds. Bringing people along, explaining the context for the decisions, and aligning and mobilizing people behind the decisions so that they were effectively involved in the decision-making process. When people are involved in the decisions that ultimately affect them, they are typically much more open to accepting and implementing them.

There is no substitute for leadership. Leaders had to stand up and be counted. At some point, leadership is needed to make any decision and ensure the decisions are supported and followed. Leaders have had to make trade-offs throughout history; this is what they are elected and paid to do, particularly in times such as these. Furthermore, leadership has to come from every layer in a business. A study in August 2020 by the Centre for Economic Policy Research and the World Economic Forum, suggested the difference between good and bad leadership is real and that it may be explained by the proactive and coordinated policy responses adopted by female leaders such as Germany's Angela Merkel, New Zealand's Jacinda Ardern, Denmark's Mette Frederiksen, Taiwan's Tsai Ing-wen and Finland's Sanna Marin.

Technology has played a role like never before. Today, data, computers, and machines are used more than ever to inform decision-making, even to the point where driverless vehicles can decide the trade-off between different life-and-death outcomes. The best organisations we work with considered how computer simulations, algorithms, and analytical tools can support their decisions with a data-driven approach.

Trade-offs shift and change through the crisis. Before COVID-19, very few of us would have predicted the trade-offs governments are making around personal freedoms. We would not have thought that we would be sharing our personal information about our locations and our medical conditions. But in less than a year, the individual trade-offs we are making have shifted markedly.

Trade-offs are becoming increasingly philosophical. More complex and existential trade-offs are addressing needs beyond the crisis, such as short-term profit compared to the planet's long-term sustainability and humanity's survival. COVID-19 may turn out to be good preparation for making these trade-offs in the near future.

Every discussion we participated in reinforced the need for sound decision-making and highlighted the role my network played with clients throughout the crisis. Many leaders knew they needed to make the decisions and trade-offs but needed a guide to weigh difficult decisions.

As always, it is valuable to consider other perspectives and learn from history. The bubonic plague forced societies to weigh the value of human life versus the day-to-day operating of society. Measures that were taken were similar to those of COVID-19, including the quarantining of the sick and the strict control over the movement of people and goods. The plague lasted four years and wiped out a third of the European population. The trade-offs that people made changed throughout the plague, and we should be prepared for the same as we deal with COVID-19.

We all make trade-offs in our everyday life. These trade-offs have seemingly inconsequential outcomes compared to some of the decisions made by governments and businesses. Yet, the foundation of these decisions is the same. Can you establish a better foundation (data, process, etc) to make informed trade-offs? What would need to change?

"It's not enough to have lived. We should be determined to live for something."

—Winston S. Churchill

PURPOSE

As the COVID crisis went on, everyone found themselves facing profound questions about their purpose. Individuals, businesses and governments considered the sheer existential function of their being.

Many of our clients are digging out and dusting off their "purpose statements" they wrote years and decades before COVID-19. For some, their purpose is more relevant and powerful than ever. Others are wondering if their purpose applies in this new world we've found ourselves in.

We have all marvelled at the organisations that have come to the fore during this crisis. We have all seen the power purpose can have in motivating people within an organisation. In the UK, the obvious example is represented through the work of the National Health Service (NHS). The sense of purpose shared among NHS employees has played a pivotal role in keeping us all safe as they worked tirelessly while risking their lives at the front line. We have known some business leaders who, themselves, experienced the care of front-line NHS workers first hand. It turns out, when you're faced with a life-threatening disease, you really start to question your purpose in this world.

Recently, the leaders we work with are getting increasingly philosophical when considering their company's purpose at a very core, fundamental level. It's nothing new; the topic has been written about for millennia. Aristotle distinguished between the purpose of fulfilling a function and a higher purpose and linked this to eudaimonia, i.e., human flourishing.

This is also resonating with employees. Even before COVID-19, a study revealed 77% of millennials stated that a company's purpose was the most important criteria for determining the companies they worked for. As our clients think beyond the crisis, individual employees, more than ever, want to work for companies with a purpose that they believe in. A recent global talent trends survey found that the highest-performing employees are 3x more likely to work for a company with a strong sense of purpose.

A common theme in these purposes? Survival. Not just survival into the next fiscal quarter or annual review, but survival in an existential, longer-term capacity. For example, sustainability is now a far more prominent purpose than we've seen in the past as our clients consider their role in decarbonisation. There is a shift from companies focusing on how to best profit from their customers to a renewed purpose in keeping them safe, warm, nourished, and secure.

Right now, to those who make up my network, purpose feels more critical than ever. It is hard for any of us to know what the world will look like in the future or how it will evolve, so we find comfort in building a purpose for today and for what we aspire to be. Businesses find it more difficult to set a direction as they come out of the crisis than they did going in, but they find that their purpose is a powerful concept to align around.

We are helping businesses revisit their purpose in a way they couldn't have imagined before COVID-19 and then helping them build out purpose-driven strategies as they move forward. The challenges of COVID-19 will be learning experiences to draw upon in the future, and purpose will surely guide the way through future crises.

With our clients, the discussions around purpose became quite philosophical. Not just in terms of their businesses' purpose, but also on topics like inherent good and whether the ultimate purpose of a species is, in fact, survival. We wondered whether an era of philosophy might be upon us and what the outcomes of such an age would be on future generations.

My network is built on aiding companies with strategy and transformation. A big part of what makes it unique is that we have a Chief Philosophy Officer who informs and guides our purpose-driven work as we stand ready to help businesses ask questions they may have never faced before.

You may not go a day without hearing about how these times are "unprecedented," and they certainly are. Those who flourish in this crisis do so because they are purpose-driven. The times may be unprecedented, but a strong foundational purpose means how you respond to challenges isn't unprecedented at all.

If someone asked you what your purpose was, how long would it take you to answer them? Is your purpose financially-driven? Or are you driven by something more altruistic?

A leader is a dealer in hope.

—Napoleon Bonaparte

LEADERSHIP

Between all the businesses we worked with through the crisis, no two shared the same recipe for effective leadership. Some leaders were thoughtful and quiet, others carried more vocal and energetic qualities, and we observed many, many styles in between the two extremes. No two were the same, but many of the CEOs and executive teams we worked with shared a few common traits.

Effective leaders are authentic. Being effective during COVID-19 had everything to do with what a leader did and said. The most effective leaders were not afraid to admit when they were wrong and were prepared to change their minds when it was the right thing to do. Effective leaders are true to their purpose.

Humility is essential. The best leaders don't take themselves too seriously. They remain humble in a way that does not come across as weak or indecisive. They keep their sense of humour about them and keep their egos under control, always ready to listen to criticism.

In the rapidly changing situations that COVID-19 brought upon all of us, the best leaders are the ones who were adaptable and flexible in their style – sometimes delegating and supporting, sometimes coaching and directing. We watched as some leaders changed their style many times over a week, or even during the course of a day, which proved crucial in a time when those around them were at various levels of competence, anxiety, and motivation. However, it is important to note that adaptability should not come at the expense of consistency and stability. Style changes, but substance doesn't.

The best leaders keep their heads and a sense of perspective. They focus on what they can control, don't worry about what they can't, and are able to stay positive because of it. Even in this challenging era, they found the time to think about the bigger picture and what is most important to them, namely their customers', colleagues' and families' safety.

The best leaders during the crisis have been seen to empathise and understand the needs of their team. They recognised when their team was anxious, when they were overly challenged at work and at home, and when they were stressed. The mood of a team is continuously evolving and changing; the best leaders are always tuned into how their people are feeling and the culture of their business.

We have seen the importance of decisiveness. When dealing with unprecedented times and there is no playbook on what to do next, leaders can easily feel hamstrung and indecisive. The best leaders never shy away from difficult decisions. Being decisive reduces anxiety in your team.

The best leaders place a high degree of trust in their teams and support them. In the spirit of Ernest Shackleton, polar explorer famed for his leadership style, these leaders "serve to lead." The best leaders support their teams. They make individuals accountable, empower them, and let them know: we're relying on you. They give their teams what they need to get through the crisis. They stand back and only step in when required. Their teams know their leaders are there for them and that they have their backs.

The best leaders show the strong values by which they live through the crisis. They stand up to what is right, and they do the right thing. They have never compromised on their values.

The best leaders set an example for others to follow. This includes maintaining a work ethic that shows their commitment while also demonstrating to their teams that it is important to look after their own physical and mental health. These leaders are in the trenches, working hard, and going the extra mile in a way that is also sustainable. And sustainability is no longer just a nice-to-have either. According to a recent survey by Glassdoor, 87% of employees expect their employer to support them in balancing work and personal commitments.

Communicate, communicate, communicate. The best leaders listen to their organisation while also ensuring that they are visible and communicative to them. Communication must be two-way and leaders must be able to receive as well as transmit. This trait also extends to customers, suppliers, and other stakeholders.

We also found that many of these points come up in some of Colin Powell's excellent lessons on leadership. Powell said that "Leadership is the art of accomplishing more than the science of management says is possible."

Colin Powell's lessons are worth reading from time to time, especially when you're facing a challenge or a crisis – such as COVID-19.

- "Being responsible sometimes means pissing people off."
- "The day soldiers stop bringing you their problems is the day you have stopped leading them. They

have either lost confidence that you can help them or concluded that you do not care. Either case is a failure of leadership."
- "Don't be buffaloed by experts and elites. Experts often possess more data than judgment. Elites can become so inbred that they produce haemophiliacs who bleed to death as soon as they are nicked by the real world."
- "Don't be afraid to challenge the pros, even in their own backyard."
- "Never neglect details. When everyone's mind is dulled or distracted the leader must be doubly vigilant."
- "You don't know what you can get away with until you try."
- "Keep looking below surface appearances. Don't shrink from doing so (just) because you might not like what you find."
- "Organization doesn't really accomplish anything. Plans don't accomplish anything, either. Theories of management don't much matter. Endeavours succeed or fail because of the people involved. Only by attracting the best people will you accomplish great deeds."
- "Organization charts and fancy titles count for next to nothing."
- "Never let your ego get so close to your position that when your position goes, your ego goes with it."
- "Fit no stereotypes. Don't chase the latest management fads. The situation dictates which approach best accomplishes the team's mission."
- "Perpetual optimism is a force multiplier."
- "Powell's Rules for Picking People. Look for

intelligence and judgment, and most critically, a capacity to anticipate, to see around corners. Also look for loyalty, integrity, a high energy drive, a balanced ego, and the drive to get things done.
- "Great leaders are almost always great simplifiers, who can cut through argument, debate and doubt, to offer a solution everybody can understand."
- "Use the formula P40 to 70, in which P stands for the probability of success and the numbers indicate the percentage of information acquired. Once the information is in the 40 to 70 range, go with your gut."
- "The commander in the field is always right and the rear echelon is wrong, unless proved otherwise."
- "Have fun in your command. Don't always run at a breakneck pace. Take leave when you've earned it. Spend time with your families. Corollary surround yourself with people who take their work seriously, but not themselves, those who work hard and play hard."
- "Command is lonely."

"We see our customers as invited guests to a party, and we are the hosts. It's our job to make the customer experience a little bit better."

– Jeff Bezos

CUSTOMER RELATIONSHIPS

We witnessed several fascinating examples of businesses that have maintained and built upon customer relationships throughout the crisis. From hospitality businesses adapting into retail outlets to fulfil their customers' needs, accounting businesses who supported their clients with COVID-19 advice, to manufacturing businesses offering good credit terms to their customers. It was amazing to see how businesses were there for their customers in a time of need.

As we reflected on these examples, we couldn't help but notice how behavioural psychology is a particularly important field of study at the moment. Businesses should understand their customers' moods, needs, and fears and use this understanding to create ways to address these needs on a practical and emotional level.

When you think about customer needs, what principles come to mind? The best businesses consider the emotional, as well as the physical, needs of their customers. They think about how their customers are feeling and how to respond to their fears and anxieties. For some of the businesses we worked with during COVD-19, we went right back to basics and used Maslow's Hierarchy of Needs as a tool to better understand what the customer needed and how they could provide for them.

The best businesses listen carefully and understand what their customers are concerned about. They make an effort to ask about their well-being and to understand how they are feeling. Furthermore, they haven't stopped listening and understanding. This is particularly important during a time when customers' needs are evolving all the time.

The Kübler-Ross grief model is particularly useful for understanding a customer's emotional frame of mind. The model talks about "anticipatory grief" with the stages of denial, anger, bargaining, depression, acceptance. Many consumers are experiencing all of these emotions, and businesses need to acknowledge these emotions as they adapt their communications, products, and services accordingly.

It has been important to consider the presence of "Battle-shock" in customers. Many customers have been experiencing greater challenges by simply processing the current situation, usually resulting in a high level of fear and anxiety. The best businesses provide their customers with a degree of normalcy, routine, stability, and familiarity.

Giving customers hope creates a strong emotional bond. Customers will always remember how businesses made them feel and the extent to which they gave them hope in the time of crisis. This has been a great way to create positive energy with customers. When the sense of hope is genuine, linked to customer's needs, and how a business fulfils the need, it ultimately strengthens the emotional connection between businesses and customers.

Telling customers that a businesses is there for them in their hour of need has proven extremely powerful. We worked with a wealth management business that phoned every one of its clients. The staff spoke to forty thousand customers, individually, just to ask if they were okay. They weren't asking about sales or expanding business; they just wanted to check in sincerely on their well-being. These calls have paid back in terms of both brand loyalty and customer retention through the crisis.

We have watched how actions speak louder than words. Being open and available for customers today will pay back dividends post-crisis. During the first and second World Wars, Coca-Cola gave away millions of bottles of Coke to US service members. It may have been difficult to place a value on this historic and iconic gesture when it happened. Still, it has since become part of the brand's American heritage.

Being honest and open with customers, especially with bad news, is something we have seen in all of the best businesses. They didn't pretend everything was normal and instead addressed the most prominent issues head-on, be they related to supply chain, financials, or whatever else. They communicated to their customers how their business had been affected by COVID-19. The result? A feeling of camaraderie, that we are all "in this together."

Successful businesses had values and purpose that aligned with their customers. According to the recent Porter Novelli/Cone purpose biometrics study, US consumers are more likely to have a positive image of (89%), trust in (86%) and be loyal (83%) to brands that lead with purpose. Nearly eight-in-10 (79%) consumers surveyed say they feel a deeper personal connection to companies with values similar to their own. And 72% say they feel it is more important than ever to buy from companies that reflect their values.

Good businesses remembered that it is okay to think commercially, even in a crisis. Actions do not have to be purely altruistic. Charging for products and services is okay. In fact, businesses find they are valued more when there is a fee involved. Yes, it has been a good time to invest in customers, offer discounts, have skin in the game, but customers understand that you are still a business in business.

Businesses realised customer relationships were in their hands; they got to decide how customer-focused they were going to be and what they were prepared to do for their customers. They also knew their competitors had the same choice. The best businesses got there first, innovated, trusted their instincts as they became extremely customer focused. This was a real differentiator in the market, and customers will remember it forever.

We heard about two local stores – one profiteered by trebling the price of toilet paper while the other maintained a normal market price.

Guess which store everyone shops in now?

Another great example was the story of a local café. The café remained open for its customers in their time of need. It adapted its products and turned their model towards retail and moved into takeaways. It started selling bread, sugar, eggs, and other staples. It became a local hub for everything you could need. The business and its owner were authentic, honest, and listened to customers. They made sacrifices and demonstrating how we are all "in it together." Today, the café is profitable and continuing to grow through the crisis. The competing café down the road? Closed.

What kind of business would you have run?

What type of practices would you have supported?

What choice would you have made?

"A man who does not plan long ahead will find trouble at his door."

– Confucius

PLANNING

There is no "playbook" when it comes to conducting business in a pandemic. We have all entered the unknown. Covid-19 has been described as a "black swan," an unprecedented and unimaginable situation with a high degree of volatility, uncertainty, complexity, and ambiguity. The crisis affects different sectors and businesses to make it hard to predict what's coming next.

Of course, this doesn't mean one cannot make a plan. Quite the opposite, in fact. Every business should have a plan. Scenario planning is an extension of this and simply builds on your traditional business plan. It can prove particularly useful during an event like COVID-19. In the short term, considering different scenarios can help align management teams around their decisions and actions, minor or major. For example, when to furlough staff, when to discontinue a product, when to retire capacity, and when to launch new products or services.

For many businesses, this stage is purely about survival.

Longer-term, once survival is assured, the principles of scenario planning can be applied coming out of the crisis and beyond. Scenario planning is a tool to test your strategy's robustness, adapt a strategy, or inform bolder, more strategic moves. This is not only about analysis but also about how your leadership team can use data, collaborate and take the right decisions.

Scenario planning is not about predicting the future precisely or even getting a rough guess at what it could be. Rather, it is about choosing potential future scenarios that may apply to your business and framing your decision making around these scenarios. As Dwight D. Eisenhower, US general and later president, said: "In preparing for battle I have always found that plans are useless, but planning is indispensable."

A key early step in scenario planning is to determine how certain external factors will affect your business. For example, the impact of social distancing on consumer behaviour and on the demand for your consumer product. There will be parts of the business that are affected positively, and others affected negatively during and after the crisis. Part of the planning is to segment your business to reflect this.

We have seen how important it is to focus on the specifics of your business and to not rely on generic predictions of the recovery. Many consulting firms and investment banks are releasing v-, w-, L-, and tick-shaped recovery type-analyses. While they may serve as helpful food for thought, every business must focus on their own situation and success drivers. The best businesses have specific, simple, practical, and pragmatic strategies and use their own business knowledge first and foremost.

Don't overthink it. Get a simple model up and running as fast as you can. The best businesses don't engage in over-complex modelling. They keep it simple and adapt as they go. They build a very simple tool that models a few key business drivers. This is the tool you calibrate during the crisis and adjust as you learn more, creating new iterations of the tool as you better understand how external trends effect your business.

Involve all functions and departments in scenario planning. The most successful businesses used scenario planning as a tool for leadership and as a communication tool within the business for determining where things stand, what has happened so far, and what might happen next. In particular, they use the planning tools to acknowledge the unexpected. They also used them to enhance people's understanding across the business and to gain feedback from the planning models to enhance and improve their understanding of what is happening.

Scenario planning is helpful for budgeting and strategy. Short-term, tactical, day-to-day decisions and immediate budgeting will likely dominate your planning. Still, businesses have found they can use scenario planning to ensure they are making "no regrets" decisions. They use scenario planning to test their strategy and take decisions in a way that makes sense across most scenarios.

COVID-19 has been a learning opportunity for thinking about scenario planning, strategy, and informing how to best run the strategy process in "peacetime." Whether they are responsible for running commercial ports, mining companies, or banks, businesses that have built scenario models that think about potential scenarios, trigger points, and decisions will have an extensive toolbox to work from once the crisis passes. They will have a better appreciation of the drivers of their business, risks, capabilities, and how to make effective decisions.

Are you planning for the unexpected beyond COVID-19? Can your planning process adapt to the reactionary way of doing things?

"Necessity is the mother of invention?"

– Plato

INNOVATION

On one of our late-night video calls, we were lucky to have a few particularly well-informed and enthusiastic participants who touched on the huge leaps in medicine, engineering, and science that occurred during and following the Second World War. We also discussed the enlightenment and the great waves of the invention that emerged from the 1650s, and the importance of the coffee shops as engines of creativity. We shared and discussed stories of exploration, military conquests, political uprisings, Silicon Valley, and financial crises. Everyone had great examples of the sheer level of innovation the COVID-19 crisis inspired, including new ways of manufacturing cheaper ventilators, new ways of doing business, the rise of contact-tracing apps, and virtual ward-rounds in the National Health Service.

It was a great session. As usual there were some useful takeaways;

Necessity really is the mother of invention. COVID-19 brought about huge challenges, but these challenges lead to opportunities. We have all confronted a new environment and have been pushed out of our comfort zones. We faced an existential challenge from being thrown into discomfort after living in a period of relative stability over the past seventy years. The conditions for innovation are ripe, and a great many businesses have adopted change and adapted to the situation. While it may have been about business survival initially, we have seen businesses move beyond this and surprise themselves at how innovative they could be. This has been as much about the state of mind and attitude as it has been about capability.

Good ideas can come from anywhere. The best ideas often come from the most unexpected places. This includes both people who are new to the business and old hands or alumni; those at the centre or at the front-line; technical experts or those with limited technical knowledge. The crisis has shown us that it is important to listen to ideas from all quarters. Innovation comes from those you least expect; it could be their time to shine, but only if we're open to listening to what they have to say.

Diversity is profoundly good for innovation. Successful innovations are drawn from people with different perspectives. Innovation thrives when people are encouraged to come together from different backgrounds, cultures, countries, business units, and functions, ultimately sharing their ideas and co-creating new ones. Technology is being used like never before to bring groups of people together. Businesses that encourage listening to others' views and building on them have innovated great ideas. We have helped our clients to collaborate with other companies too, even fiercest rivals.

Start with the problem and work backward. A product looking for a need rarely succeeds. Innovation is most effective when it first focuses on a customer need or a problem that needs to be solved and how to solve it. Innovative teams quickly develop a solution that might work and then build on and iterate it to something that can be implemented. They then look at how to build on their solution to create other ideas and add value to the customer. When businesses address a problem that causes customers difficulties, the solution invariably adds value to them, and the business has prospered.

Leadership either catalyses or kills innovation. We've watched leaders engender a culture that is conducive to innovation by challenging the status quo, trusting and empowering people, elevating the good ideas, giving people a licence to innovate, and ultimately empowering their teams. The best leaders made everyone feel they can make an important contribution. They have encouraged networking, broken down the silos, and disrupted the hierarchy while ensuring they are visible and are communicating openly. The crisis has been an unsettling time for most; anxiety is not the best state to innovate from. It has fallen to leaders to reassure and support people more than normal.

Revitalize Your Toolbox. Given the pace that recent innovations have needed to come about, we've seen excellent examples of companies using their existing technology and finding ways to adapt it to the changing conditions. Oftentimes technology is combined and mixed to serve entirely new purposes. Great businesses don't assume innovation necessarily means inventing new technology; there is merit in being resourceful and using what you have. Just take a look at the renewed role video conferencing has taken in every business during this crisis. And the most innovative companies are going beyond the basics. The companies on BCG's most innovative list for 2019—especially those in the top ten—extensively use AI and innovation platforms.

Just do it! Taking risks is fundamental to innovation. "Fail fast, fail well," while a cliché, is totally on point. Test-and-learn. Get the ideas off the paper and into the market, then adapt and improve later. Learn from feedback, adapt and adjust, and go again. Businesses with a rapid cycle of iterating ideas get ahead of the competition quickly.

The right incentives matter. That is, the broadest sense of the word "incentives." Businesses that set up the conditions for a culture of innovation have thrived. It's not just about monetary rewards; it could simply be about recognition and making sure innovations are celebrated. Businesses thrive when they reward success and risk-taking. All of this extends to innovation conditions on an elementary level, including location and physical space. If the physical conditions are right, innovation is more apt to happen and can even be enhanced by a COVID-19 environment. For example through new connections enabled by technology.

Strive for a learning organisation. The best businesses have been learning from the COVID-19 crisis while they endure it. These are hugely formative times. Every day there are hundreds of new findings and experiences to learn from. Learning from them will be valuable both now and in the future. The best businesses have reviewed and documented their successes and failures. From what we have observed, the winners have already started discussing how to avoid the trap of falling back into old habits once this crisis passes.

Despite the importance of innovation, many businesses still find it hard and do not think they are good at it. According to a recent McKinsey Global Innovation Survey, although 84% of executives agree that innovation is important to growth strategy, only 6% are satisfied with their innovation performance.

How do you translate the innovations of COVID-19 into "peacetime"? What we're experiencing now will be hugely valuable in the future. The best businesses realise their people live with high levels of uncertainty and are getting used to constant change and adaptation, and are using this to learn how to be flexible, adaptable, and innovative. This ought to make their businesses more resilient and successful in the future. How can we re-create the urgency and creativity of the COVID-19 crisis once it is over?

"Talent wins games, but teamwork and intelligence win championships."

– Michael Jordan

HUMAN RESOURCES

The way COVID-19 spreads and its impact mean many business challenges are very much people-related. When it comes to people and human resources, every business faces extreme challenges. Some are planning for more than eighty percent of roles in their companies not being required during the crisis, some are preparing for staff reductions of more than thirty percent, others are considering a workload increase of more than fifty percent. In many businesses, upwards of ninety percent of people simply cannot work from home for one reason or another.

Many of these organisations are operating across multiple countries, each with different regulations, and each at a different stage in the crisis. In every case, there is significant uncertainty as supply, demand, and people-driven constraints change daily.

In talking with clients and associates, two points rang through the clearest: 1) having a robust people plan is vitally important, and 2) so is your ability to adapt creatively. The best businesses in just about every case highlighted the following ideas:

Prioritisation: The clear business priority is in the safety of their people. Additionally, they ensure human resources and resource planning are a priority for the crisis coordination team.

Constraints: They establish a clear base of facts that social distancing and other COVID-19 guidelines apply to their business during the crisis. This will vary by local area, region, country and could change daily. They ensure this information is updated frequently, disseminated, and factored into decision-making throughout the organisation.

Demand: They understand what drives human resource requirements and monitor how the crisis affects these. For example, whether there is an increase or decrease in everything from manufacturing volumes, retail sales, online sales, and the effect this has.

Supply: They understand the impact that the constraints will have. They consider the compounding of multiple constraints on the availability of people. Employees who are off sick *plus* employees caring for others *plus* remaining employees being less productive *plus* an additional workload *plus* new capabilities and skills that are required.

Dynamic planning: It's one thing to have a robust and thorough plan, but make sure it is dynamic enough to update as the situation changes. Good businesses think in terms of possible scenarios, phases, and what could potentially trigger them. They use these scenarios to drive their decision-making. They pay attention to details, including equipment, consumable requirements, and training, including these in the planning process.

Innovation: They think creatively. They encourage innovation throughout the organisation and have everyone engage with both the problem and the solution. They are willing to think of things in completely new ways, using this as an opportunity to challenge old structures and methods for a post-COVID-19 world. They remember that this is temporary, it will pass. For example, they may satisfy another, totally different customer need during the crisis. Or they might consider not releasing employees from the business but into temporary roles in the market that may only exist during the crisis.

Support: They empathise with people. Remember that some people are finding the state of the world more difficult to adapt to than others. This is not just a work-related crisis; it extends into personal, social, and family lives. The best businesses offer advice on maintaining mental and physical well-being and encourage their employees to speak up if they are struggling to cope. It is always worth considering how to use your business's resources to support the team.

Open communication: Great businesses are becoming learning organisations as they review outcomes from COVID-based decisions and learnings. They communicate clearly, frequently, and consistently. They are open and honest with their people about the options they have and the impact of the decisions they are making.

Invest: Great businesses realise their people will remember how their employer treated them during this crisis. They make sure not to lose the human touch as they make business decisions involved with human resource planning. They keep checking in with their people, staying abreast of their personal situation, and making sure they are coping and being supported where possible. Not only is this the right thing to do, but it can affect morale, retention, and culture for years to come.

Under all of the businesses and governments and organisations are people. Our greatest resource. What can you do today to nurture this resource?

What can you do, today, to nurture yourself?

"If everyone is moving forward together, then success takes care of itself."

– Henry Ford

MOTIVATED TEAMS

*E*very one of our clients, without exception, is struggling with keeping their teams motivated during this crisis. Without the routine, structured environment of the workplaces we are used to, and with the added stress of staying healthy and safe amid a pandemic, some teams feel more lost than others.

This is important as it has a huge impact on the success of businesses. Research by Bain & Company concluded that if a satisfied employee's productivity level is 100%, an engaged employee's level is 144%, but the productivity level of an employee that is truly inspired is a whopping 225%.

Our clients are taking all kinds of different approaches to engage and motivate their teams; here are a few of the major success points we've observed.

Prioritise safety, welfare, and well-being. Put the team first, but do not neglect to look after yourself. If you are fit and healthy, you are more likely to be in a positive frame of mind and better able to support your teammates. Encourage others to do the same.

Over-communicate. Keep the team informed with simple

messages. Less is more. Avoid jargon. Don't hide bad news; share it even if you don't have all the answers. Let the team know what is being done to pursue answers and solutions. Inversely, communicate successes and positive developments, however small they may seem. During difficult times, hearing about success stories from other parts of the business can be highly motivating.

Empathise with the team. Put yourself in their shoes and take time to listen. Understand how they are feeling. Invest time to understand team problems and share their importance across the team. According to a recent survey by Salesforce, the software company, employees who feel their voice is heard are almost 5 times more likely to feel empowered to perform their best work.

Provide structure. Establish routines for the team so that you are making frequent check-ins. Keep the drumbeat going. Maintaining a rhythm will break up the day, keep people motivated, and ensure they are more positive, confident, and productive. Have a plan that includes short-term goals and a future vision that emphasises a positive outcome.

Celebrate positive behaviours. Especially for team members who are thinking positively and trying new things, even if they do not always succeed. So long as they are done for good reasons, and the team can learn from them, celebrate it. Acknowledge failures but point out the positives and the lessons. Everyone on the team should share both successes and failures.

Use facts and information. Be open and honest with people. Minimise conjecture, opinion, and hearsay so you can focus on the truth. Be clear on what is known versus assumed to inform decisions, vision, direction. Use the facts to consider future scenarios and help you to plan and prioritise. A common basis of understanding will build confidence and positivity. Understand what you cannot control and focus on the things you can.

Play to each other's strengths. Allow team members to find a role that allows them to make a positive contribution. Draw on people's experiences and capabilities. Ensure team members feel they are in a role where they are contributing. Keep a lookout for team members who are not prepared for their role and who need support. Empower and encourage the team to deliver. Know when to support them and when to get out of their way.

Maintain an oasis. Make sure you and the team have retreats and safe spaces where they can step away from work and put the crisis out of mind for a moment. Furthermore, make it clear that you *want* them to do this from time-to-time. This could be as simple as getting away from the front line or out of the team room, taking a walk (even if around the house or workplace!), calling friends or family, or switching off your email notifications. Even just a few moments of calm can bring an immense feeling of relief.

Use and encourage humour and laughter. Banter, jokes, stories, observations that are self-generated or generated by others. Don't take yourselves too seriously. Keep your sense of humour and encourage others to do same.

Think about how to measure levels of positivity and motivation. This could be extremely basic, by simply asking people how they are feeling and why. Ask the individual, and ask the group, perhaps trying more formal surveys or feedback. Test the mood and see how you can improve upon the results. We're in the middle of a pandemic crisis and emotions are tough to deal with; bringing awareness to the problem is the first step. Showing an authentic interest in making things better is the difference between a motivated, productive team and one that is not engaged.

Link motivation to purpose. If a business has a strong

purpose then motivation of employees becomes a lot easier. According to a recent survey by Great Place to Work, employees who report that their job has a "special meaning: this is not 'just a job'" are 4 times more likely to give extra, 11 times more committed to staying with their organisations and are 14 times more likely to look forward to coming to work than employees at peer companies.

Ask, honestly, what it would take for your team to leave? Better wages and benefits? A better work environment? Then consider why they stay. What could you do to increase theirs, and your own, motivation?

"It is really wonderful how much resilience there is in human nature. Let any obstructing cause, no matter what, be removed in any way, even by death, and we fly back to first principles of hope and enjoyment."

— Bram Stoker, Dracula

RESILIENCE

We had one particularly good video call around the theme of resilience. We heard fascinating examples of how teams and people were resilient during the crisis, including the NHS, a team working on the reconstruction of Iraq, the perspective of an ultra-long-distance swimmer, several military examples, and the thoughts of a pair of round-the-world yachtsmen.

Resilience can be defined in many ways, but in this context, it best includes preparedness, responsiveness, reliability of a business's systems and processes, levels of redundancy and backups, resourcefulness, adaptability, flexibility and, most importantly, attitude.

Attitude is everything. Crises like COVID-19 can bring out the best in people, but only with the right attitude. We all observed huge changes to the businesses we work with. Even in the presence of extreme pressure, stress, and anxiety, we saw teams channel these emotions into exceptional outcomes by keeping a positive attitude.

Having a plan is important, but not sufficient. Good decision making, teamwork, and being able to deal with the unexpected while adapting the plan are all more important than having a plan alone. When faced with the choice of investing time in making plans versus building team behaviours in "peacetime," make sure sufficient time is spent on the latter.

You can't fake it. The underlying culture of a team is fundamental to determining how they will perform when they are backed against the ropes. The National Health Service in the UK is a good example showing how a culture of communication, coordination, prioritising, and teamwork was already business-as-usual but is now coming into its own during the crisis.

A business does not suddenly become resilient. Resilience is developed and learned through experience. How a team works together during smaller challenges determines how they will respond during a wide-scale crisis. How you perform on the smaller stage prepares you for the main event.

How you respond is key. Airline crash investigators will tell you the cause of most aviation disasters is not mechanical failures. Rather, the cause is in the cockpit. The effectiveness of the response during an in-flight crisis determines the survival rate of the passengers. This all comes down to remaining calm, drawing on training, working together, communicating, and adapting to the situation as new information appears. It is not about how you got into the shit, but rather how you get out of it that matters.

A team is only as strong as its weakest link. Identify how people on your team respond to different situations. Observe who comes into their own during the COVID-19 crisis. Look for people who adapt, innovate, stay positive, step-up, and lead – they are the ones you want on hand during the post-crisis days. Inversely, keep an eye out for weak links and support them or move them into roles where they can thrive.

Resilience is a source of competitive advantage. In a crisis, some businesses cope far better than others. How well your business copes is a competitive advantage when "peacetime" comes back around.

Don't wait for a crisis. Based on the many examples we reviewed, the organisations that struggled during COVID-19 already had cultural issues before the crisis. In particular, hierarchical, overly structured, and check-list driven organisations with a lack of empowerment and accountability struggled the most.

Resilience can be enhanced through routine. Sticking with a routine brings about huge benefits to an organisation in a crisis. Routine has been linked to positive thinking and maintaining motivation, which allows leaders and their teams to make good decisions.

Leadership is fundamental to resilience. Not just at the top, but the leaders throughout an organisation are essential. Leaders should be visible and give clear communication to enable people to be positive, try new things, and feel like an empowered part of the team.

In the conversations we had throughout the crisis, an organisation's resilience determined how they dealt with the existential threat of COVID-19 and also how they plan to respond to other crises, such as climate change or financial threats. In all, the resilience of tomorrow starts today. The COVID-19 crisis has been altitude training for whatever challenges organisations face next.

"If you want to go fast, go alone; but if you want to go far, go together."

– African Proverb

COLLABORATION

Collaboration has proven to work and to create exceptional value during the crisis. We've seen loads of examples where several organisations brought their talents and resources together to create a result greater than the sum of their parts. In particular, we see a huge value in diversity in its broadest sense, including diversity of thought, experience, and expertise.

Collaboration is an active choice. A willingness and desire to collaborate is the starting point; collaboration requires someone to take the first step. You won't know the value of your collaborative projects until you explore the opportunities with others. To some extent, businesses who successfully collaborate started with an active mindset and first decided they will collaborate, and then they worked out the "what" and the "how." COVID-19 ended up being a great catalyst for collaboration.

Openness is the starting point. Be open, have conversations, discuss opportunities, and share information. Each party must lower their guard and reach out to others. Trust is essential.

There must be a shared purpose. This may start from a customer need or a problem and could result in a new product, service, or technology. Whatever your purpose, identify it early on.

All parties must benefit. Incentives to collaborate and create must be aligned across all participants. However, these incentives do not need to be monetary. There is plenty of incentive in building a reputation or altruistically doing the right thing.

Establish a framework. Principles, ground rules, and a framework are foundational to effective collaboration. You may not need them at the outset, but they will be necessary before too much investment occurs. Be clear on what you are trying to achieve, what the boundaries are, and what processes you will use.

As always, leadership is critical. A key part of this is giving your people "permission" to collaborate. Don't just let them know it is okay to collaborate with others, but celebrate and reward their collaborative endeavours. Communicate success stories and publish examples to encourage others to do more of the same.

Embrace technology. Many businesses find that Zoom, Teams, Hangouts and other video conferencing technology enable effective long-distance collaboration. Distance is no longer a barrier to bringing ideas together. And there are a plethora of other tools for working together more effectively that are now available such as Slack, Trello and Discord

Consider what you can contribute beyond your core business activity. COVID-19 resulted in a huge amount of spare capacity and unused capabilities. Spend some time working out what these are, you never know what hidden assets may now be valuable in a way you haven't thought before.

Collaboration is not easy. Many people talk about it but

not nearly as many who actually do it. Be prepared for collaboration to take a lot of energy and effort from you and your organisation. But it will be worth it, and it can really pay off. One of the best examples we saw was the coming together of British industry to design and build life-saving ventilators in just seventy days from a standing start.

Collaborating when there is an obvious crisis seems like a given. The question stands: will we continue to foster collaboration in the post-pandemic world, where it may be even more important? How do we ensure we do so?

"Clients do not come first. Employees come first. If you take care of your employees, they will take care of the clients."

– Richard Branson

WELL-BEING

*A*cross my entire network - from independent consultants to businesses large and small all around the world - the well-being of employees and their leadership has been an all-important topic.

The COVID-19 crisis only exacerbated an issue that was already critical during normal circumstances. 2020 has been a rollercoaster year for everyone; emotions are all over the place; there are heightened anxiety and stress levels both at work and in the home.

There are multiple layers to the causes and effects of well-being. At the most direct are the effects of the disease, both immediate and the longer-term impacts we still don't understand entirely. According to a recent study, one in five people infected with COVID-19 develops mental health issues as a direct effect of the disease. Beyond that, there are the indirect effects of lockdown, including financial concerns and social isolation.

The best businesses demonstrate that you have to care. Aside from being the right thing to do from an ethical, duty-of-care point of view, caring for your employees' mental and physical well-being drives several aspects of business performance, including customer service, productivity, efficiency, and enables businesses to function effectively. Well-being also helps to drive recruitment. According to a recent report by the American Psychological Association, 89% of workers at companies that support well-being initiatives are more likely to recommend their company as a good place to work. Well-being affects everyone and there is both a moral and contractual obligation to take it very seriously.

We're all paced differently. We are all on an emotional curve at different points every day. We found it useful to imagine that we and everyone we interact with is dealing with their unique position on this curve. Furthermore, people may be on more than one emotional curve at the same time. For example, one curve applies to their work situation and another for their personal circumstances, one for their immediate team and one for the business they work with. It's a lot to juggle.

There have been several phases of COVID-19. The first was highly emotional – stressful, challenging, terrifying. Many of our clients were running on adrenaline as we dove into crisis mode. Most found it scary and challenging; others found it invigorating and even exciting. Adrenaline got us through it. Additionally, the first phase happened in the summer, at least in the northern hemisphere, which is an easier time of year to maintain both mental and physical health.

Subsequent phases have been quite different. In the next phase, we all saw the adrenaline wear off, and a new state emerge. Emotional exhaustion and fatigue set in. People were tired, and it may have affected how they continue to respond to COVID-19. Then, a third phase began. People could see some light at the end of the tunnel. Coming out of the crisis requires a hugely different approach than we saw going into it. It will be confusing. It will feel harder to consider the implications of our decisions and to think about strategy. Minds are foggy, and there is still significant anxiety. This will test us in entirely new ways and affect what employees and leaders build into the future, particularly as we go through the winter months.

There is limited data. Medical professionals already see a wave of mental health issues among their patients. Many people will admit to having faced mental and physical well-being challenges throughout 2020. It is a personal thing, and it affects people in vastly different ways, but it is proof of how deeply this crisis had affected everyone.

Whatever the issue, it is good to talk about it. Already in the run-up to COVID-19, more discussions were happening around well-being. We can now speak much more openly about the issue than we might have a few years ago. While most of our clients were already thinking more about employee well-being before the crisis, they focused on it even more during 2020 as they sought to maintain safe working environments and ensure ongoing physical and mental well-being.

In our video calls, we shared several tips to help maintain a safe level of well-being:

Don't stay glued to the news all the time; take time to relax, and make sure you step away from Zoom or Teams now and again. Think about how to be healthy in body and mind. Eat well, maintain good sleep habits, be careful of alcohol levels, and get out of the house when you can. Have face-to-face meetings (masked, socially distant, outdoors) when you can. Keep a routine and get some exercise. Get a dog. Or a cat. Or an iguana. Most importantly, find out what works for you. Also, leaders: don't forget to look after yourselves as well as your teams.

Discussions on well-being also highlighted how some

people are ready to return to the office, and others are still wary about working in public. Businesses are investing in how they move forward safely. Money has been spent on the office, including moving furniture, installing plastic screens, and re-configuring the layout to make employees feel safe. Testing is administered each week. Leadership has been more visible as CEOs have been communicating, getting out into the business, and listening to their employees. Beyond this, businesses have new collaboration tools to facilitate conversations and invest in counsellors, mentoring, and support.

Our resident Chief Philosophy Officer noted how the leader's behaviour in the workplace significantly affects employee well-being. A recent study concluded that good leadership, including leaders who motivate their teams, inspire them with a clear vision, and communicate well, can reduce anxiety in employees.

Moving forward, in "peacetime," well-being will be a priority for employees. But will it stay a priority for your business?

"Hope is being able to see that there is light despite all of the darkness."

– Desmond Tutu

COMING OUT OF LOCKDOWN

*A*ll of our clients have begun to think about how to come out of lockdown mode at the end of this pandemic. Since early in the crisis, some have been thinking about it, planning for the short term and thinking about how to build back better.

It turns out that it is harder to come out of lockdown than it was going in. How do you take the lessons learned in COVID-19 and apply them to the next phase?

While every organisation we work with was hit extremely hard by the crisis, we saw their teams working more effectively, achieving amazing results, and ultimately working better as a team than ever before. In particular, all of our clients have seen a level of collaboration and a team spirit across their organisation unlike anything they have experienced pre-COVID, with business units and functions working together in ways that they had previously not thought possible.

Leadership has been a theme in every scenario, with leaders stepping to the fore and being visible, empathising, communicating well, and inspiring those around them. As a result, many of our clients achieved results they would previously have thought impossible, including accelerating projects and programmes that might have had timescales of many months or years and achieving these in just weeks or even days.

Specific examples include how they moved one hundred percent of office workers to work from home over the span of a weekend, reducing travel budgets by ninety-five percent overnight, reaching out to every single customer in a fortnight, moving entire product and service portfolios online in just a month, transforming a restaurant chain into a shop, designing and building ten thousand ventilators from scratch, and keeping the shipping industry moving. And, of course, the development and rollout out of vaccines.

Every project was taken in stride. But to achieve this, organisations had to adopt project management tools, daily video calls, online communication, and other simple processes that enabled their teams to deliver in a more effective way than ever while also working remotely.

Most organisations now have the time to debrief, discuss, and document their lessons from lockdown in detail. They have identified the people, behaviours, and processes that enabled them to get through the crisis and noted what newfound abilities they don't want to lose. They have seen a side of their organisations which they have not seen before, and they want to retain the behaviours for when the world returns to business-as-usual.

The process of coming out of the crisis feels more daunting than it was going in. Businesses are foreseeing even greater levels of uncertainty, bigger challenges, and more ambiguity. The lessons from the crisis will be necessary for whatever the next stage holds.

As they think about the future, all of our clients are evaluating the extent to which they should return to their previous business models versus adopting the new ones. Supply chains are being re-evaluated, profit pools are being reassessed, business models examined, and strategies reviewed. In many cases, clients are asking questions about their businesses that they never asked in the past.

Even though the situation is unprecedented, the fundamentals still hold. These include the importance of safety, the need to focus on the customer, the increasing importance of technology, the importance of talent, and the need to provide value.

There are no precedents for this next phase of the crisis; it is as though we are learning how to walk again after coming out of a coma, starting an engine again after it being idle for years. We can use dozens of analogies, but they all point to needing to negotiate the next phase carefully, so we come out of the crisis stronger.

The world we knew before the pandemic is largely unavailable to us. Moving forward, with everything we know and have experienced, what kind of world would you want to work and live in and what can you do to shape this?

"Learn from yesterday, live for today, hope for tomorrow."

– Albert Einstein

BONUS CHAPTER: THE FINAL LOCKDOWN?

My network has now spent more than a year working with organisations as they navigate through the different phases of COVID-19. We continue to draw on the many years we have each spent helping businesses through other challenging periods, developing strategies and running transformation programmes.

As of February 19, 2021, the COVID-19 outbreak had been confirmed in over 210 countries or territories. The virus had infected around 110 million people worldwide, and the number of deaths had reached over 2.4 million.

As the crisis continues, we continue to hold regular video calls to share our experiences and publish key points from our discussions in case they are useful for others.

On our most recent call we discussed "lockdown 3" which in many countries, including the UK, is defining the next phase of the crisis. We are helping small and large businesses across multiple industries and geographies right now, so we had a good discussion. As ever we captured the key points.

We compared the approaches our clients are taking as the crisis continues and as they continue to face short-term challenges and, increasingly, consider post-COVID-19 strategy and "building back better". At the time of writing it is hoped that this will be the final lockdown in the UK. Time will tell …

Going into "lockdown 3", many leaders and their teams are tired. After repeated cycles of lockdown-relaxation-lockdown without a break, working with heightened stress levels, fatigue has now well and truly set in and is a key characteristic of this latest phase. In some businesses this is translating into negativity. A survey by IPSOS-Mori of c1,000 executives found that six in ten Britons in January 2021 say they are finding it harder to stay positive day-to-day compared with before the virus – an 8-point increase from November 2020.

The crisis is a lot more real for people this time round. One person on the call remarked that numbers have now become names for many people. For the first time on these calls, we each knew at least one person that had died with COVID-19. Someone on one of my teams suffered the death of a family member last week and another told of several deaths of people she knows. A former colleague sadly lost his wife. We are all concerned for family and friends and the daily statistics continue to be alarming.

Working from home and home schooling is much more intense this time round. All the kids are at home now, the days are more demanding, the younger ones in particular need more support and parents are more stretched. Granted, not everyone is affected by this, but it does affect a very large proportion of decision-makers and doers in all businesses, and has a knock on effect on their teams and the people around them. Other groups have equivalent challenges and many are side-tracked and thinly spread.

While employers are certainly taking steps to look after their teams, it is hard to make sufficient allowance for the additional demands, for example ensuring deadlines are realistic and that sufficient support is being provided to help teams work effectively. Teams are told that mental welfare is important, to take care of themselves, to take the time to home school … but are then still required to deliver that urgent report by Monday.

There is a high level of uncertainty about how long "lockdown 3" will last. Psychologically, many people can't see the light at the end of the tunnel. They don't know when we will be back in the office, when gyms, pubs, restaurants or shops will open or when kids will be back at school. This makes it hard to plan or to look forward to a time when we return to a more sustainable and normal situation.

It's January! The weather and short days have compounded the mood. Christmas has been very different has felt like a long weekend to many with insufficient time to recharge before getting going again. Many people had expected the post-Christmas period to be one of opening up and improvement whereas it has been the opposite and expectations have had to be adjusted. This has already gone on longer than we thought and people are adjusting to this being an 18 month stint and not a 6 month. It is as if we started a race thinking it was 10km and found out that it is actually a marathon. The glass feels half empty. In the same IPSOS Mori poll, just 45% of Britons expect life will return to normal this year.

It can actually be harder to come out of a crisis than it is going in. Teams ran on adrenaline last year. The focus was on pure survival in many cases. Now businesses have to take a measured view on the future and consider how to plan in a world of uncertainty with a wide range of outcomes. There could be lockdowns 3, 4, 5, … There could be tiers 6, 7, 8, 9, … The vaccine may kick in in weeks … or months. But we have to plan and taking each day as it comes doesn't work when businesses have to take investment decisions. it is harder than ever to plan and teams haven't the bandwidth, energy or capabilities to consider a highly complex situation.

The UK is particularly challenged right now compared to certain other countries. A survey by the leaders council of GB and NI found that 89% of respondents felt that New Zealand is doing a better job of handling the crisis. Countries like NZ and Australia are back to normal. We have spoken to people there, and also in Taiwan recently. In these markets, business is continuing. Although there are other countries that are struggling, the success stories make the situation in the UK feel even worse, by contrast.

Admittedly the situation is somewhat downbeat, but we are a constructive group and we see a lot of positives on the projects we are currently working on.

The good news is navigating the next phase is largely in our own hands. We continue to help businesses to respond to ambiguity and uncertainty with clarity and decisiveness. Many of our clients have been highly agile and innovative. In particular small businesses, but also large ones. We are helping companies to take decisions, make plans, assess scenarios, run meaningful strategy exercises. There is much that other businesses can learn from these examples of best practice.

Another positive is that we have seen huge advances in behaviours and culture. We have seen teams come together through the crisis. Teams are flatter with fewer silos, and managers trust their teams more. There are great examples of online collaboration, and collaborative technology. We have been involved in remote-managed projects that wouldn't have seemed possible in the past.

"Lockdown 3" continues to be a learning opportunity that many businesses are seizing. How businesses respond when their backs are against the wall is fascinating. We are seeing how it is possible to train an organisation to become more resilient, to become more innovative. We are also seeing how to influence the psychology and culture of an organisation. We are seeing the importance of being open, collaborative and using data.

Our resident philosopher reminded us that this is a great time for people to reach out beyond their team, department or company to get through this phase. Key and Co is a good example of this, bringing experience of managing through crises, developing strategies and leading transformation programmes, for example. We have also found we can bring skills from beyond the business world through our network, from the military to endurance athletes.

As I write, more than 15 million vaccines have been distributed and the lockdown exit plan is being finalized. The sky is blue and the spring is coming. Businesses are beginning to look ahead to the future. There is much to be hopeful for.

EPIGRAPH

"The greatest glory in living lies not in never falling, but in rising every time we fall."

– Nelson Mandela

EPILOGUE

Everyone, and no one, predicted the COVID-19 crisis.

Virologists from around the globe warned of a major outbreak for years. The wake-up calls of SARS, MERS, and Ebola were nowhere near as loud as they needed to be. Even as children, many of us heard about the great plague of the 1300s – we knew the power the microbe had when it came to causing widespread upheaval, death, and destruction. I have seen the words "global pandemic" on the corporate risk registers of many, if not all, of the large businesses that I have worked with during my career.

Still, few people thought it would happen or were planning for it. Few predicted the year that we have just had. In fact, as 2019 ended, many were anticipating a prosperous and plentiful year in 2020. Businesses were optimistic, projecting growing revenues across most sectors and geographies.

To say 2020 was a surprise doesn't do it justice. Now, as the year draws to a close, we are looking back to reflect on what happened and how to take stock of the impact and

EPILOGUE

properly digest the lessons. The results may take many years to analyse.

There is a great benefit to capturing these thoughts, reflections, and lessons while still fresh in mind; this book has attempted to do this. It is not, and cannot be, anything approaching a comprehensive account of 2020 or the COVID-19 crisis. Rather, it is a series of observations from one group of people, working with businesses throughout the year and documenting their thoughts and reflections. If anything, I hope you find it helpful and that it might even trigger some of your own reflections.

I wish you good fortune in 2021.

Good luck and stay safe.

Jon Key,

Key and Co Ltd.

ACKNOWLEDGMENTS

With thanks to all in the Key and Co. network.

Especially to Alessandro, Anna, Ed, Feisal, Jacqui, James, John, Jossie, Lorcan, Manny, Mark, Martyn, Paul, Peter B, Peter L, Russell, Sam, Simeon, Stu and everyone else who joined our late-night video calls.

And of course, thanks to my tolerant and supportive family! Ali, Edward, Eliza, Isy and Ned (and Coco). And Mum, Dad and my brother Tim.

Also, thanks to David, Doug and Henry for helping to turn our musings into this book.

And finally, of course, thank you to all of the key workers that have worked to keep us all safe through the crisis.

ABOUT THE AUTHOR

Everyone has their story about how the COVID-19 crisis changed their life. These stories start long before the rollercoaster that was 2020 started, and each perspective was shaped by experiences we shared long before the virus struck.

I was born in 1974 in Cambridge, where I grew up with my parents, Carol and Bill, and my brother Tim. I am a "towny" and a "gowny," having also studied engineering at Cambridge University.

After obtaining my master's degree, I stuck around Cambridge for a hugely informative post-graduate year where I studied design, manufacturing, and management by visiting hundreds of companies, small and large, both in the UK and worldwide. The experience gave me a curiosity for business, which has stayed with me ever since.

I have spent my career both as a consultant and in a series of executive roles with public and private companies, while also running my advisory business. I specialise in solving critical and complex challenges with CEOs and their leadership teams.

Over the years, I have developed an extensive network of clients, colleagues, and friends and bring them together into teams with the experience and expertise to solve the most challenging business problems.

Along the way, I have taught English in China, competed in a Cambridge-Oxford lightweight boat race, taken part in a round-the-world yacht race, and run in ten marathons. I have lived in Australia, Africa, Asia, Europe, and South America and have been lucky to travel to many exciting places and meet some extraordinary people.

I draw my inspiration and energy from my hugely talented, and somewhat eclectic, global network. I am fortunate to have my family's support; my wife Ali, children, Edward, Isy, Eliza, Ned, and our dog, Coco. We all live together in London, one of the most exciting and diverse cities in the world.

I passionately believe in learning from life's experiences – my own, and the experiences of others. Like each of you, I have had my own share of ups and downs, and I look for lessons from every experience that I can apply to new and future situations. The COVID-19 crisis has been especially enlightening and granted us all a plethora of new experiences to learn from. I've observed many people going through more downs than ups and have found myself with a renewed commitment to learning. This book is part of that quest.

linkedin.com/in/jonkey

GETTING IN TOUCH

I hope you have enjoyed reading this book. Please get in touch if you would like to learn more about our global network of consultants and advisors. I would also be delighted to hear your own lessons from the crisis.

Website: www.keyandco.org.
    Email: corporate@keyand.co.

www.ingramcontent.com/pod-product-compliance
Lightning Source LLC
Chambersburg PA
CBHW030445220526
45464CB00006B/2423